Animal Journeys

Migrating with the
Wildebeest

Thessaly Catt

PowerKiDS
press™

New York

Published in 2011 by The Rosen Publishing Group, Inc.
29 East 21st Street, New York, NY 10010

First Edition

Editor: Amelie von Zumbusch
Book Design: Ashley Burrell

Photo Credits: Cover, pp. 4, 5, 7, 14, 16, 19 (top, bottom) Shutterstock.com; p. 6 © RFCompany/age fotostock; p. 8 Dmitri Kessel/Time & Life Pictures/Getty Images; p. 9 (top) Tim Graham/Getty Images; p. 9 (bottom) James Warwick/Getty Images; pp. 10–11 Paul Souders/Getty Images; p. 12 © www.iStockphoto.com/Paul Banton; p. 15 © Panorama Media/age fotostock; p. 17 © www.iStockphoto.com/Jocrebbin; p. 18 © www.iStockphoto.com/Peter ten Broecke; p. 20 Daryl Balfour/Getty Images; p. 21 Mitsuaki Iwago/Getty Images; p. 22 © www.iStockphoto.com/Josiah Garber.

Library of Congress Cataloging-in-Publication Data

Catt, Thessaly.
 Migrating with the wildebeest / by Thessaly Catt. — 1st ed.
    p. cm. — (Animal journeys)
 Includes index.
 ISBN 978-1-4488-2544-8 (library binding) — ISBN 978-1-4488-2795-4 (pbk.) —
 ISBN 978-1-4488-2796-1 (6-pack)
 1. Gnus—Juvenile literature. 2. Gnus—Migration—Juvenile literature. I. Title.
 QL737.U53C38 2011
 599.64'591568—dc22

                                        2010028194

Manufactured in the United States of America

CPSIA Compliance Information: Batch #WW11PK: For Further Information contact Rosen Publishing, New York, New York at 1-800-237-9932

Contents

The Wildebeest's Journey

Some animals make long journeys every year. These animals often travel along **routes** that members of their **species** have taken for thousands of years. This kind of journey is called a **migration**. Animals migrate for many reasons, including to keep safe from **predators** and to find food or warm weather.

These wildebeests are migrating across Tanzania's Ngorongoro Conservation Area. This land is on the route of the wildebeests that migrate between the Serengeti Plain and the Masai Mara.

Wildebeests live in south, east, and central Africa. They migrate throughout the year to find fresh grass and clean water. Many wildebeests migrate each year between the Serengeti Plain, in Tanzania, and the woodlands of the Masai Mara National Reserve, in Kenya. Some wildebeests travel over 1,000 miles (1,600 km) on this yearly migration.

Wildebeests can be found in many parts of Africa. Some wildebeests live in Africa's hot, dry deserts. This wildebeest is in the Kalahari Desert in South Africa.

Black and Blue Wildebeests

Black wildebeests, such as this animal, have coats that are darker and heavier than those of blue wildebeests.

Wildebeests are members of the antelope family. Species in this family have hooves and long, thin legs. There are two kinds of wildebeests. The first is the black wildebeest, also called the white-tailed gnu. The second is the blue, or common, wildebeest. Blue wildebeests are generally gray or brown, with a black mane and tail. They have black stripes on their shoulders.

Wildebeests can weigh up to 600 pounds (270 kg). Both male and female wildebeests grow horns. Wildebeests have a long row of sharp teeth that make eating mouthfuls of grass easy. They can live for up to 20 years.

These are blue wildebeests. Blue wildebeests are also known as brindled gnus.

African Plains and Woodlands

Blue wildebeests live in the grassy plains and woodlands of south, east, and central Africa. Wildebeests need to drink water two times a day, so they are never too far from

This huge herd of blue wildebeests is making its way across the Serengeti Plain.

bodies of water. The millions of blue wildebeests that spend the rainy months of November through March on Tanzania's Serengeti Plain are often called the Serengeti wildebeests. Many people call their migration between Tanzania and Kenya the great migration.

These wildebeests live in the Ngorongoro Crater, in Tanzania. The crater is home to many animals.

These wildebeests are in Kenya's Masai Mara National Reserve. The northern part of the Serengeti wildebeests' yearly migration is inside this park.

Black wildebeests were once heavily hunted by people. The animals almost died out. However, farmers and parks made room for wildebeests to live. Today, they are making a comeback.

These migrating wildebeests are starting to cross the Mara River.

Right: The red, orange, and yellow arrows on this map show the general route that the Serengeti wildebeests travel each year.

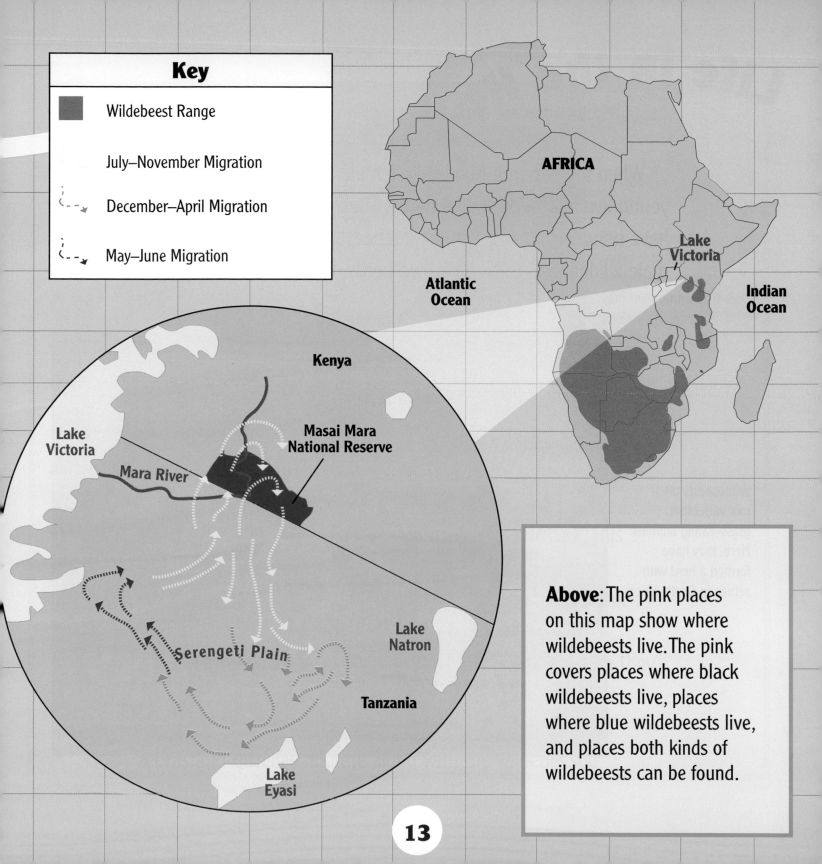

Key

■	Wildebeest Range
	July–November Migration
	December–April Migration
	May–June Migration

AFRICA

Lake Victoria

Atlantic Ocean

Indian Ocean

Kenya

Lake Victoria

Mara River

Masai Mara National Reserve

Serengeti Plain

Lake Natron

Tanzania

Lake Eyasi

Above: The pink places on this map show where wildebeests live. The pink covers places where black wildebeests live, places where blue wildebeests live, and places both kinds of wildebeests can be found.

Wildebeest Calves

Wildebeest calves, such as these two, spend a lot of time running and playing with other calves.

Male and female wildebeests **mate** each year in May and June. The females have babies, called calves, sometime in February or early March of the next year. More than 500,000 wildebeest calves are born in just two or three weeks. This is called a **synchronized** birth.

Wildebeest calves can stand about 6 minutes after they are born. After a few days, they can run fast enough to keep up with their herd. They follow their mothers to keep from getting lost or killed by predators. Calves drink their mothers' milk until they are about six months old. When they are about 10 days old, they start eating grass, too.

A wildebeest calf will stay with its mother for about a year before going off on its own.

Many Predators

Wildebeests have many predators. Lions, leopards, cheetahs, hyenas, and African wild dogs are among the animals that hunt wildebeests. Crocodiles **attack** migrating

This big cat is a leopard. Leopards are powerful hunters. Wildebeests are among the animals that leopards most often hunt.

wildebeests when they cross rivers. Predators often hunt young wildebeests rather than adults. This is because adult wildebeests are very fast. They can run away from predators at more than 50 miles per hour (80 km/h). Young wildebeests are much slower and weaker.

The crocodiles that most often hunt wildebeests are Nile crocodiles, such as the one charging at these two wildebeests.

Wildebeests are among the fastest animals on Earth!

The zebras that travel with migrating wildebeests have very good sight and hearing. Young wildebeests watch the zebras to see if they become scared. This is how they know a predator is nearby.

Wildebeests and People

Each year, many people travel to the Serengeti National Park, in Tanzania, and the Masai Mara National Reserve, in Kenya, to watch the Serengeti wildebeests on their yearly migration. Some people even follow the migrating wildebeests, zebras, and gazelles on trips called safaris. People like to watch the wildebeests as they climb over hills, run through valleys, and cross rivers.

People on safaris often ride in off-road vehicles. This lets them reach animals quickly and watch them safely. The people in this vehicle are looking at wildebeests in the Masai Mara National Reserve.

This man is filming, or making a movie of, a wildebeest. You can learn a lot about wildebeests by watching movies made of them in the wild.

However, people also cause problems for wildebeests. For example, some people put up fences around their land along the wildebeests' migratory route. This **disrupts** the wildebeests' migration. Farmers also use the water that wildebeests drink to water their crops.

Protecting Wildebeests

Many wildebeest **populations** across Africa are declining, or getting smaller. In fact, the Serengeti wildebeests are the only population of wildebeests that is not in decline. **Climate change** is also a problem for wildebeests. It causes changes in weather, such as the amount of rain that falls during the wet season.

Serengeti wildebeests are doing fairly well. Much of the land they migrate through is parkland. People did not fence it in, so animals can migrate through it.

However, many people want to **protect** wildebeests. There are **conservation** groups working to make sure wildebeests have places to live and enough food and water. Hopefully, wildebeests will keep making their yearly migrations for years to come.

Glossary

attack (uh-TAK) To charge at.

climate change (KLY-mut CHAYNJ) Changes in Earth's weather that were caused by things people did.

conservation (kon-sur-VAY-shun) Doing something that looks after nature.

disrupts (dis-RUPTS) Changes something in an unsettling way.

graze (GRAYZ) To feed on grass.

mate (MAYT) To come together to make babies.

migration (my-GRAY-shun) The movement of people or animals from one place to another.

populations (pop-yoo-LAY-shunz) Groups of animals or people living in the same place.

predators (PREH-duh-terz) Animals that kill other animals for food.

protect (pruh-TEKT) To keep safe.

routes (ROOTS) The paths people or animals take to get somewhere.

species (SPEE-sheez) One kind of living thing. All people are one species.

synchronized (SING-kruh-nyzd) Done at the same time.

territorial (ter-uh-TOR-ee-ul) Guarding land or space for one's use.

Index

Web Sites

Due to the changing nature of Internet links, PowerKids Press has developed an online list of Web sites related to the subject of this book. This site is updated regularly. Please use this link to access the list:
www.powerkidslinks.com/anjo/wildebee/